From Cement to Bridge

From Cement to Bridge

Ali Mitgutsch

Carolrhoda Books, Inc., Minneapolis

LIBRARY OF CONGRESS CATALOGING IN PUBLICATION DATA

Mitgutsch, Ali.
  From cement to bridge.

    (A Carolrhoda start to finish book)
    Edition for 1979 published under title: Vom Zement
zur Brücke.
    SUMMARY: Follows limestone from the quarry to the
factory where it eventually is formed into cement and
ultimately becomes concrete and is made into a bridge.

    1. Bridges, Concrete—Design and construction—Juve-
nile literature. 2. Cement—Juvenile literature. 3. Concrete construction—Formwork—Juvenile literature.
[1. Concrete. 2. Cement] I. Title.

TG335.M5713 1981   666'.893   81-334
ISBN 0-87614-148-3   AACR1

      1 2 3 4 5 6 7 8 9 10 86 85 84 83 82 81

From Cement to Bridge

Cement is made from limestone and clay.

Limestone is a kind of rock.

This is a limestone **quarry**.

Limestone is taken out of the quarry
and sent to a cement factory.

At the factory the limestone and clay are put into a large machine called a **crusher**.
The crusher grinds the limestone and clay into smaller pieces and mixes them together.

Then the mixture is put into a large furnace
called a **kiln**.
Inside the kiln the temperature
is almost 3000°F (1600°C).
This heat changes the mixture
into a substance called **clinker**.
The clinker is in pieces
about the size of marbles.

When the clinker is cool, it is crushed one more time.

It is put into a large, round metal container.

Inside the container are thousands of steel balls.

As the container turns around,

the steel balls crush the clinker into powder.

This powder is called **cement**.

The cement is stored in paper sacks
or in large silos until it is used.
Cement is used to make **concrete**.
Concrete is a thick paste that is made
by mixing cement with gravel, sand, and water.
When concrete dries,
it becomes as hard as rock.

Here are some workers
building a frame for a bridge.
The frame is made of wood and steel.

The concrete is poured into the frame.
Then it is left to dry.

In a few days the concrete is dry.
The wooden frame can be taken down
and people can use the bridge.

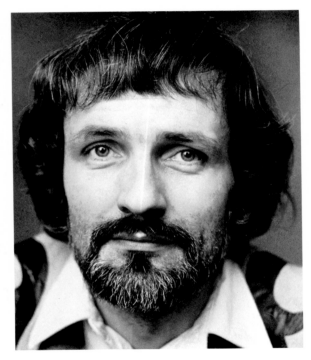

Ali
Mitgutsch

ALI MITGUTSCH is one of Germany's best-known children's book illustrators. He is a devoted world traveler, and many of his book ideas have taken shape during his travels. Perhaps this is why they have such international appeal. Mr. Mitgutsch's books have been published in 22 countries and are enjoyed by thousands of readers around the world.

Ali Mitgutsch lives with his wife and three children in Schwabing, the artists' quarter in Munich. The Mitgutsch family also enjoys spending time on their farm in the Bavarian countryside.

THE CAROLRHODA

>>> START

From Beet to Sugar

From Blossom to Honey

From Cacao Bean to Chocolate

From Cement to Bridge

From Clay to Bricks

From Cotton to Pants

From Cow to Shoe

From Dinosaurs to Fossils

From Egg to Bird

From Egg to Butterfly

From Fruit to Jam

From Grain to Bread

From Grass to Butter

From Ice to Rain

From Milk to Ice Cream

From Oil to Gasoline

From Ore to Spoon

From Sand to Glass

From Seed to Pear

From Sheep to Scarf

From Tree to Table

TO FINISH >>>
BOOKS